An Anthology

Surviving Her

Finding Hope Beyond the Pain

Empowered by Cathy Harris
Co-Authors: Cheryl A. Bruce   Tonya Dale
Maryann R. Dannert   Shant'a Miller
Natalie Purdie   Stacey D.M. Shaw
Kiana L. Stallworth   Chiezda Washington

SurvivingHer™ – Finding Hope Beyond the Pain, An Anthology
By Cathy Harris
Co Authors: Cheryl Bruce, Tonya Dale, Maryann R. Dannert, Shant'a Miller, Natalie Purdie, Stacey D.M. Shaw, Kiana L. Stallworth, Chiezda Washington
Copyright © 2020. All rights reserved.

No part of this book may be reproduced to transmitted by any person or entity, including internet search engines and retailers, in any form or by any means, electronic or mechanical, including photocopying, recording, scanning or by any information storage and retrieval system without the prior written permission of the author of this book.

Scriptures marked KJV are taken from the KING JAMES VERSION (KJV): KING JAMES VERSION, public domain. Scriptures marked NIV are taken from the NEW INTERNATIONAL VERSION (NIV): Scripture taken from THE HOLY BIBLE, NEW INTERNATIONAL VERSION ®. Copyright© 1973, 1978, 1984, 2011 by Biblica, Inc.TM. Used by permission of Zondervan. Scriptures marked TM are taken from the THE MESSAGE: THE BIBLE IN CONTEMPORARY ENGLISH (TM): Scripture taken from THE MESSAGE: THE BIBLE IN CONTEMPORARY ENGLISH, copyright©1993, 1994, 1995, 1996, 2000, 2001, 2002. Used by permission of NavPress Publishing Group. Scriptures marked NKJV are taken from the NEW KING JAMES VERSION (NKJV): Scripture taken from the NEW KING JAMES VERSION®. Copyright© 1982 by Thomas Nelson, Inc. Used by permission. All rights reserved.

This anthology reflects the various author's present recollections of experiences over time. Some names and characteristics have been written, some events have been compressed, and some dialogue has been recreated. The advice and strategies found within may not be suitable for every situation. This work is sold with the understanding that neither the author's nor the publisher are held responsible for the results accrued from the advice in this book.

Trade paperback ISBN: 9798670628396

Dedication

To my Lord and Savior Jesus Christ for planting such a beautiful vision inside of me to help women restore their lives and share their powerful stories.

Acknowledgments

To Natalie, Stacey, Maryann, Shant'a, Kiana, Chiezda, Tonya, and Cheryl for having the courage to share your stories so others can have hope.

To all women who are struggling in your circumstances and afflictions, may you see something in these stories of survival and from them find the courage and strength to live a life free from chains and strongholds. May these heartfelt intimate testimonies demonstrate to you, that you too have the strength to walk in your authentic selves.

I want to express my thanks to Monique Jewell Anderson of Spirit Filled Creations for everything, whose wisdom and experience helped guide us through the complex journey of getting this book published and bringing everything together.

Table of Contents

Introduction 6

Cathy Harris 13

Cheryl A. Bruce 17

Tonya Dale 29

Maryann R. Dannert 41

Shant'a Miller 59

Natalie Purdie 75

Stacey D.M. Shaw 91

Kiana L. Stallworth 107

Chiezda Washington 123

Introduction

Surviving means continuing to exist, remaining intact. SurvivingHer an anthology is a window into the world of women who have survived and have overcome life experiences as seen through their eyes. These women were brave enough to face their demons, battle them, and come out on the winning side. Their stories are a powerful moving testament of courage, compassion, and above all, the will to survive.

Within these pages of SurvivingHer, you will find remarkably unique accounts that will leave you inspired, encourage, motivated, and empowered. Each contributing author offers insight into a moment that changed her life forever. They faced challenges, adversities, loss, overcoming fears, and circumstances that held her back in some way. They did not walk away untouched, but rather they did so with renewed strength and wisdom.

Surviving Her – Finding Hope Beyond the Pain

Many of you have gone through something. If you have not gone through anything, just keep living. Life can get extremely hard sometimes and we might wonder if God is even there. Trauma, brokenness, generational curses, low self-esteem, low self-worth, stagnation, insecurities, the need for validation and approval, and so much more will steer you in the wrong direction and keep you there if you don't deal with the actual root of the problem that lies within you.

The first step in surviving anything is dealing with "YOU." We can be our own worst enemy. Yes, things will happen to us, and it might not be our fault, but what happens afterward is still up to us. Second, realize exactly who the enemy is. Our battle is spiritual. The devil will use people and our past to make us think badly about ourselves. Negative self-talk is high on the devil's list for seeking and destroying who God says we are. But the devil is a liar.

Surviving Her — Finding Hope Beyond the Pain

Do not believe anything negative the enemy or others say about you. Do not allow them to let your past destroy your present and future. Third, replace every lie you are told with the truth. Silence everything in your mind that is negative or hurtful that says that you are not enough. No matter what you are going through, God loves you and HE will help you turn pain into gain. Everyone has a past and goes through something. We cannot let our past define us.

Recovery is a process. Recovery requires constant and intentional acts of honesty. One must be willing to talk about old wounds and current pains. Think about how your restoration can help change your life, your family dynamics, and the lives of others. Your testimony is for someone else. Removing your mask allows for the authentic person to come out. Doing this will take some time. Peeling back the layers of lies you believed and accepting who you truly are will not be easy. However, in

SurvivingHer — Finding Hope Beyond the Pain

doing so, realize what is unique about you and celebrate your uniqueness.

Remember you are not like anyone else. God in his sovereignty sets you apart. I have learned to live my life unapologetically. Learn to be okay with saying no, set boundaries, and balance family and work. Your journey will also require you to regularly examine your circle of influence. Not having the right people in your circle could hurt your journey to being who you truly are and living the life you have been called to live.

In every heartfelt chapter of SurvivingHer, that I have the honor to introduce, you will witness God showing up and showing out. Every woman's truth will touch your soul. I wholeheartedly believe sharing their story was part of God's plan.

SurvivingHer is for anyone struggling to get their life back, or for anyone looking for hope and inspiration. The detailed accounts in SurvivingHer are more than just

Surviving Her – Finding Hope Beyond the Pain

survivor stories, they are a compelling tribute to the enduring quality of the human spirit.

Maya Angelou once said, "There is no greater agony than bearing an untold story inside of you!"

Use our stories to give voice to your own.

Cathy Harris
National Motivational Speaker
Best-Selling Author
Christian Counselor
Degreed Life & Business Coach
Advocate for Domestic Violence and Rape
Philanthropist

Surviving Her ANTHOLOGY

Finding Hope Beyond the Pain

Empowered by

Cathy Harris

SurvivingHer Founder: *Cathy HARRIS*

Cathy Harris

Brings with her over twenty years of leadership development experience. Cathy is a bestselling author, Christian counselor, dynamic motivational speaker, philanthropist, life, and business coach. To Cathy, all these titles stand for a servant for God. Teaching cutting-edge life skill strategies and uncompromising integrity are the hallmarks of Cathy's service to help women recover, walk-in their authentic calling, and share their stories. Cathy has a passion for telling her story and sharing the tools she used to not only survive but thrive. Cathy is a domestic violence and sexual assault advocate who provides messages of hope, motivation, encouragement, empowerment, and inspiration. Cathy encourages people to find their voice and use life's stumbling blocks to rebuild their lives. She is the CEO and founder of the award-winning 501(c)(3) nonprofit organization MyHelpMyHope Foundation. Cathy advocates, assist women and children in crisis situations, and fights for social justice through her nonprofit organization. She is

Surviving Her — Finding Hope Beyond the Pain

the CEO of Kingdom Coaching & Consulting, a company that provides affordable life coaching to those who want to reach their maximum potential in life and business. Through one-on-one coaching, group coaching, and custom presentations, she uses proven techniques to help women find fulfillment in doing what they love. Cathy is the recipient of numerous award including the Wavy TV Channel 10 Who Care Award, the Zeta Phi Beta Sorority Finer Woman Award, Hampton Roads Gazeti Exemplar Award, ACHI Magazine Woman of the Year Award, ACHI Magazine Philanthropist Award, Genieve Shelter Hero Award, and the Garden of Hope Unity Award from Gethsemane Community Fellowship Church. Cathy's work has been featured on the nationally syndicated Dr. Oz Show. Wavy 10 News, 13 News Now, and WTKR Channel 3. Cathy has also been featured in publications such as the Virginian-Pilot, the New Journal and Guide, the Hampton Roads Gazeti, and Tidewater Women. The MyHelpMyHope Foundation was recently selected as a change-maker by the Obama Administration in 2017, Michelle Obama, and Oprah Winfrey. Cathy has

Cathy Harris earned an AS in psychology, a BS in Christian counseling, a BS in life coaching, and a BS in addiction and recovery from Liberty University. Cathy is currently earning her Master's Degree in Mental Health Professional Counseling.

Websites: thecathyharris.com
screamsfromthechurchpew.com
Facebook: @cathyharris and @coachcathyempowers
Instagram: @coachcathyempowers
Email: coachcathyharris@gmail.com

Cheryl A. Bruce

Founder of The Admin Suite, is a savvy administrative professional with 35+ years' experience. She supports a wide range of industries that include legal, real estate and event management just to name a few. With her personable personality and calm demeanor, she is the right hand to your left; the pleasant to the "straight to the point."

She also serves as Chief Administrative Officer for Destined to Be Free, a Domestic Violence and Abuse Awareness Organization. Here she can be a voice and advocate for victims and their families.

In her free time, she enjoys her grandchildren; a good glass of wine; live jazz music and shopping for the funkiest pair of 5-inch heels she can find!

I Walked Into It, God Brought Me Through It!

After eight and a half years and a heated conversation, I decided to put an end to the relationship with my boyfriend, he on the other hand, did not agree with my decision. Feeling the need for a witness, I was going to call my mother when he grabbed it from me and threw my cell against the wall, cracking it. He then locked the bedroom door. Fear crept in as he had threatened to harm me before. Then, for the very first time, the unthinkable happened. He told me to take off my clothes. I refused. Then piece by piece – first my blouse, then my lace brazier, my jeans, my underwear – all ripped off my body. I don't know if it was already in his hand, but somehow, he whipped me on my thighs with an extension cord. I screamed and pleaded with him to

Cheryl A. Bruce

stop, but that just made him more enraged. I was alone in the house and terrified for my life. I tried to fight back, but he overpowered me, threw me to the floor and began choking me. I don't know how much time passed because I just remember opening my eyes to see him sitting on the side of our bed looking pissed. When he realized I wasn't dead, he yelled, "Get up." He dragged me by the arm and pulled me into the bathroom. While plugging in the nearby iron he filled the sink with water. "Put your fucking face in the water." At that moment, all I could think was God I don't want to die like this. Then I heard a voice say, "Fight!" How? What am I supposed to do? I was weak and quite frankly, petrified. As he grabbed my neck to push my face into the water, I heard the voice again, fight. In a split second, I had the heated iron in my hand, and I was swinging it toward his head as hard as I could. Startling him, I was able to break away and run down the stairs as fast as I could. I just knew he was right behind and I was right. Still naked, I hid in the laundry room attempting to find clothes so that I could sneak out

Surviving Her — Finding Hope Beyond the Pain

of the backdoor. But there was no need, carless, I heard him on this phone trying to get a ride and saying, "She's going to call the police." I heard my front door open, then closed. I peeked out of the window and saw him walking towards the corner. I prayed, thanked God, and just as nothing happened, I showered, dressed, and picked up my granddaughter to take her to an event I had promised she could attend. I never shared with anyone what happened, I just continued with my daily routines and told myself that I was perfectly fine.

I didn't see or speak to him for months. I did, however, receive constant texts and voice messages. He started off very apologetic, but the more time that passed between calls, he reverted to his usual mean and ugly self. He belittled and threatened me and spoke ill of my family. One day, I received a call from a hospital advising they had admitted him, and he needed emergency surgery. They listed me as his next of kin, and they needed some key medical information related to his condition. My first instinct was to provide the staff with his family's contact information, but my soft heart said, "Cheryl, don't withhold something that could save his life." I gave them what they needed. The next day I received another call -it was him. "How are you?" I asked. We talked for quite a while. As the days and months passed, I remained cordial. I answered his calls every now and again. I figured if I did not answer regularly, he would understand and move on too. But time taught me he and I didn't think the same – at all.

New Year's Eve.

"Hey, what are we doing tonight? Whatever it is, let's do it together." He said.

"Ah, that's a no, from me. I don't think it's a good idea we continue to talk. I think you're getting the wrong idea from our conversations."

He exploded and yelled, "I'm gonna kill you."

Surviving Her — Finding Hope Beyond the Pain

Although it had been nine months, his words took me back to that day and I felt helpless all over again. I hung up and curled up on my sofa, and just laid there. I trembled every time my phone rang. I just couldn't move. Each year my family usually got together for the occasion, but I was apprehensive. He could have been outside my door without my knowledge. I called my mom and made up some excuse why I wasn't coming over. I heard the disappointment in her voice, but she did not pressure me. Little did she know, I was allowing fear to take over me and keep me away.

I had a regularly scheduled appointment with my pulmonologist, I remember him saying to me "I don't know what's going on in your life, but I think you need to get help because with what I'm seeing your oxygen levels were extremely low - you shouldn't be alive." I wasn't alive, at least I didn't feel like I was. I felt like I was just existing and putting on the biggest front so no one would know what was going on with me. He asked me if I felt

Cheryl A. Bruce

safe at home. My answer was yes, which was a lie. He asked me if I needed to seek therapy and I said no. The last thing I wanted to do was to talk to someone about why I allowed my boyfriend to abuse me the way he did. I was the tough one, I took no stuff off anyone. I could not let anyone know that I was mentally beaten down, depressed, and wanted to just go hide in a corner. I had an image to protect.

His behavior only got worse. He started leaving me messages about what I wore to work, what time I left the building for lunch, and when I got home in the evenings. He was stalking me. I went to work and not leaving out of the building until it was time to go home. Then I would get home in the evenings and immediately go straight upstairs and lock myself in my bedroom. I would sit in the dark and if I saw headlights shine near the house, I would get down on the floor and crawl over to the window to peek out to see if it was him. When I had conversations with my mom or my kids, I made sure I sounded as upbeat

Surviving Her – Finding Hope Beyond the Pain

as I could. I never wanted to let on to them that I was living as a prisoner in my own home. I never wanted them to know I was afraid of being there by myself. There were a few occasions I would pack a bag, put in my trunk, and make up some excuse for my mom to go to her house and sleep there. By this time, I think she knew something was going on but never questioned me. Her concern was I was safe. She would just let me rest because I was worn out. The things I did became my normal.

It was summertime, but for me, the livin' had not been easy. I was tired, I was broken, but I knew this couldn't be what God had for me. I had retreated from the things I loved to do, and I was missing out on life. I no longer traveled, entertained friends, or enjoyed social outings. But one morning, I woke up and said enough was enough! No more going back and forth, no more talking to him, no more being afraid, no more. I got up with a pep in my step and headed to the courthouse. I filed the paperwork and had a court date set.

Cheryl A. Bruce

I knew the exact time he received the paperwork because he blew up my phone, continually calling my cell and my office. Between both lines, he left 72 messages telling me to leave town if I knew what was good for me; that he didn't care who I told because he wasn't afraid of anything happening to him if I died.

When I had my day in court, I realized that the system sucked. I had 72 messages saved to a flash drive and the judge would not even hear my case. My boyfriend was still hospitalized, and the judge used his excuse for a postponement. As tears begin to fall, one of my friends who is an attorney spoke up for me. After all the legalese speak, the judge heard the matter and issued the restraining order. Miraculously, the next day, he was released from the hospital and showed up at my job.

He came running across the street and grabbed my arm. Why would you file a restraining order against me? Empowered, I said, No sir, not this time. I looked him in the face and said you are not supposed to be near me

Surviving Her — Finding Hope Beyond the Pain

because according to the piece of paper I have in my purse, a restraining order was granted. That was the last day that I saw him. After months, I could finally breathe in relief.

Ironically, five years later from that day I lay on the floor with his hands around my neck, I received a phone call saying he was dead. I didn't shed any tears of sadness, only relief. At that very moment, I was ready to reclaim my life. Not the life I lived during that 8 ½ years, but the life that God had planned for me.

My healing process took some time to begin but during that time, I learned that to push past my pain; I had to forgive him and myself! Him for the way he treated me and myself for the continual blame that I placed on me for staying in a relationship where someone hurt me.

I know now that the pain I experienced was preparation for me to begin the walk into my purpose. The purpose of using my voice to encourage others in letting them know

Cheryl A. Bruce

that whatever you're going through, even if God didn't bring you to it, He will bring you through it!

I'm more determined than ever to make each day *Amazing on Purpose*.

Email: Cheryl@CherylBruce.com
Website: www.CherylBruce.com
Facebook: @Cheryl Bruce
Instagram: @Cheryl Annette Bruce

Tonya Dale

Is a notable humanitarian, mentor, and business entrepreneur. She is the owner and executive director of Empowered Women of Virginia, Inc. (EWOV) a non-profit organization. EWOV assists women facing homelessness, domestic violence, and release from incarceration.

Tonya has received numerous awards for her humanitarian efforts such as the 2013 Black Entrepreneurship Award for Outstanding Dedicated Service in Hampton Roads, 2016 Exemplar Award, 2017 Chesapeake Redevelopment and Housing Authority Award, 2017 J. Cox Elementary School Award, 2017 Hearts Full of Grace Award, and the 2018 VIP Women's Empowerment Tea Award. Tonya has dedicated her life to helping women reaffirm their power and potential through accountability, prayer, mentoring, and motivation.

My Purpose Was In My Pain

Growing up, I hated women. Mostly because at six I was sexually and physically abused by an adult friend of the family. She was so close to us that we called her a cousin. And then a visit turned into my mom announcing she was moving in. I believe at that time she began grooming me. She knew I would trust her because I was a child. I felt special because of all the attention she was giving me. She was very affectionate with kisses and hugs – when we were together, she held me close to her. My mom was a single parent of four and my sister Tawanda was special needs. I felt neglected, so when the cousin offered me some attention, I took it. The physical attention escalated into her asking me to do things to her like touching her private area. I knew what she was asking me to do was wrong, so when I cried, she stopped…temporarily. One day as my mom was leaving the house, I begged to go with her because I was afraid of what usually happened when my momma left. My cousin grabbed my arm and pulled me into her, "you're not going anywhere." When I heard our front door close, I nearly peed on myself. I was so afraid of her. Whenever my mom was away, she called me in her bedroom, and she made me do unthinkable things. She made me put my mouth on her vagina and made me lick her. That was the first time I saw hair in the private areas of a woman's body. I begged and pleaded with her that I didn't like it and I didn't want to do those nasty things. If I refused, she would beat me with her fist, belt buckles, and anything else she could grab. She would punch me in my face and then lock me in a closet for hours and I would beg to come out. She would say the only way you come out is if you do what I tell you. I did sometimes because I was so afraid of the dark. This was torture for a six- and seven-year-old child. This woman would beat me in my head and there were

Surviving Her — Finding Hope Beyond the Pain

times I had bruises. My bedwetting and my stuttering began. I couldn't say one word without stuttering. I became very angry and felt a lot of rage at times. I felt nasty most of my childhood. As a child, I would pick on my sister Sonya. I would make her cry by fighting her because she was so happy all the time. I was so jealous of my special needs sister because she got all the attention. I began lying and stealing. I was angry and did things so someone would notice me too. I would think about killing my abuser because she wouldn't stop. At eight, she moved out, and I was so happy, I thought this would never happen again because the devil was out of my home. It happened again with men touching me. I became numb to it.

As a teenager, I hung out with older men. I became curious about sex and wanted to know what it was all about. I wanted to know why everyone loved it so much. The older men could see that I was very naïve, and they took advantage of me. I hated sex; I didn't get what was so good about it. I felt dirty.

Tonya Dale

I married my first love at the age of twenty-one and we had two beautiful children, Victor Parker Jr, and Felicia Parker. I knew nothing about anything. I was in love and that's all that mattered. In hindsight, we were too young, and I had some serious issues such as rage, trust issues all stemming from my childhood. Even though I married my first love I still had issues with sex. I loved this man, but I wasn't healed from what happened as a child. He hurt me and I couldn't get past the pain, so I left him, and we later divorced.

By my late twenties, I hung out with a lot of men because in my mind they wouldn't hurt me. But they did, because I was raped three times. I blamed myself and felt so ashamed. As time passed, I didn't care about anything anymore except my children. I did whatever I wanted to do and didn't care what anybody said. I was reckless. I slept around and I wanted to give up on life. I wanted to die. I was angry with God and my momma. Both had the opportunity to protect me, and neither of them did. I had thoughts of suicide daily. I got into relationships that meant me no good and I could not see the bad because all the dysfunction was my normal. If things were going right, I left the relationship because in my mind if it's going right then it's not right.

My second marriage happened because he reminded me in some ways of my father. In the beginning, He was loving, very attentive to my needs, and he adored my children. However, two weeks before I was to marry him, things started to happen. Women were calling my phone, telling me they were in a relationship with him. Some even threatened me and when I told my friend about them, they begged me not to marry him. I even received a warning from the Lord. He said so clearly, "This man is not your husband." But I married him anyway because I loved him and thought he'd change because of me. He was an addict. I understood how my mother felt. I understood those nights she was crying and fighting. We had just purchased a new home and then I got sick. I had a pain in

Tonya Dale

my side, and I went to the local ER. That one visit lasted two weeks in the hospital because of an infection on my ovaries and a high fever. I had one visit from my husband and his friend. I followed up with my primary care Dr., she informed me that there was something on my ovaries and they wanted to do a biopsy. The results showed I had ovarian cancer. The cancer doctor informed me they had to remove both of my ovaries because the cancer had spread – which led to a hysterectomy. Disregarding the doctor's instructions, I went back to work because we needed my income. I had been bleeding for an entire year and told no one not even my doctor. Then one night on my way to work, I passed out at the light because of blood loss. I woke up, and I was scared to death. I went through all this alone. Then we lost the house.

My pain turned into a deep depression. There were days I couldn't get out of bed. One day while in my bedroom, thoughts ran across my mind about how I would take my life. I just wanted out of all the pain. I thought about my

Surviving Her — Finding Hope Beyond the Pain

children and I knew that my death would hurt them deep but my pain was deeper. I thought that I was going crazy. I couldn't function - I was drinking alcohol and smoking weed every day, all day- just to feel normal.

One day while sitting in my room the Holy Spirit whispered in my ear and said, "Just leave." That was the pivotal moment in my life that I knew it was time for a change. It was as if I was given courage at that very moment. The feeling of unconditional love and boldness came over me. I jumped out of my seat and realized I wanted to live. It was as if I had a job to do and no one would stop me from doing it. I was determined to get it done.

August 1st was the day of my new beginnings. I left this man and never looked back. Empowered Women of Virginia Inc was born. God gave me the Vision for my Nonprofit Organization. My Mission is to help people who are in need. The Lord told me to provide for my Brothers and my Sisters of All nationalities. My

Tonya Dale

Organization saved my Life and gives me great pleasure in serving my community. Three years later, God sent a man that I met twenty years prior. And even then, he told me I would be his wife, but I laughed because I couldn't see it. When we reconnected, he made his intentions clear that he wanted to spend the rest of his life with me, but trust and believe I didn't make it easy. He loved me just as I was flaws and all. Today we are happily married, and I thank God daily for sending me my husband. He is the true definition of a Godly man. He loves me for me.

I sought counseling for my childhood trauma. Counseling was the best thing I could ever do to heal all the pain. I read inspirational books, I meditate, I surround myself with strong women who lift me up, encourage me, and hold me accountable. That's something I never had from a woman.

I am no longer ashamed of my past and now I have Purpose. My Purpose was in my pain. I am no longer bound by my past. *I am free* and I owe it all to God, he

Surviving Her — Finding Hope Beyond the Pain

gets all the *glory*. He is still holding me down and I am a better woman today. My favorite quote that I use daily is from Maya Angelou "My mission in life is not merely to survive, but to thrive; and to do so with some passion, some compassion, some humor, and some style."

My biggest hope for humanity is to feed, clothe, heal, and educate the world. Lord, thank you for keeping and loving me through all the crazy things I have done. Thank you for giving me so many chances. Thank you for giving me the visions, thank you for sending my Boaz, Troy Dale. My life is so fulfilling today. I am so happy, and I wouldn't change a thing because it made me the woman I am today. *My name is Tonya Dale and I am a woman empowered.*

Tonya Dale

Facebook @ewovainc
Instagram @ewova_inc
Email: ewova2012@gmail.com

SurvivingHer Author: Maryann R. DANNERT

Maryann R. Dannert

Is the Fearless Living Coach © and a Human Resources Professional. As a Certified Life Coach, her life's mission is to empower, inspire and motivate women from coast to coast, to gain self-confidence as they create the life, they've always desired: a life where they are free & happy, living life on their terms.

In overcoming adversity, she has turned her life around and the once high-school dropout holds a Master's degree in Leadership and a Bachelor's degree in Organizational Management. She is also a three-time published, best-selling author. Maryann's story, not yet completely written, continues to unfold. Embracing her fearless and fabulous spirit, she currently resides in the state of Florida and she enjoys the beach, traveling, and spending time with her family.

A Letter to My Dad

A couple of my favorite television shows growing up were Different Strokes, Who's the Boss, and The Cosby Show. You know what all those shows have in common and what they taught me about daddies? Dads should be affectionate, loving, and protective of their daughters. I didn't have that. Those images taught me that fathers are to shield their daughters from harm.

I have written this in my head and on paper many times. I write, I read; I delete… I self-criticize and then – I begin again. This time, I will write, I will breathe and through the tears, I will finish. I no longer worry about what others will think or say because I've held back for far too long. Keeping such things inside paved the way for me to

Maryann R. Dannert

transition from a broken girl, into a rebellious teenager who grew into a woman that was distrustful and cautious – a woman that was not the real me.

Dear Dad,

I'm sitting here on the balcony, overlooking the water, trying to gather my thoughts as I write this letter. I'm at a conference at work and we've taken a break to work on an exercise, which is supposed to help us be better leaders – and ultimately become part of a healthy team. The facilitator has spoken about how our past experiences shape our thought process, behaviors, and personality. As the instructor spoke, I knew this would be a difficult assignment, as we must dig into our past, face our fears head-on, and create a plan to move forward. All of this made me think of you.

I thought of all the times we missed – times that I wanted to share with you. When you and mom divorced, I was

Surviving Her – Finding Hope Beyond the Pain

only about three, and it seemed like you divorced me too. Living in Puerto Rico, I rarely saw you and then, after we moved to Rochester, NY, you were non-existent.

Do you know that my favorite colors are pink, purple, and teal? Pink reminds me of innocence and femininity, purple is royalty, power, and strength, and then there's teal – my love of the ocean – which is peaceful, safe, and comforting. I remember one day being at the beach and it was such a beautiful and perfect day. The sky was clear, and the sun was shining brightly. The air was fresh and warm. I think that's when I fell in love with the ocean. Do you even know how much I love the ocean? How could you – you've never asked on the rare occasions that we spoke. Anyways, hearing the waves crashing against the shoreline, felt safe and I did not want to leave. It was peaceful. The peacefulness was broken when I tasted the saltwater, nearly chocking. It was supposed to be you teaching me how to swim and not another man. It was

Maryann R. Dannert

your shoulders I was supposed to be on as I was taken into the water, inch by inch.

What about my athletic abilities – do you know about those? In elementary school, I loved running and almost every race I ran in, I came in the top three. And in middle school, I loved playing volleyball and basketball. Then there was high school – life was about to change, and not for the better.

I do remember you visiting me and picking me up to go spend time with you. But the visits were brief and felt cold. You also seemed to be preoccupied with other people, instead of spending time with me – getting to know me. It seemed like you were fulfilling a moral or perhaps legal obligation. While you should have been asking me questions about how things were going or teaching me and guiding me about life – the do's and don'ts, you were busy showering me with gifts, but I didn't feel loved or wanted. For those reasons, I never opened up to you. For those reasons, you never knew what happened to me.

Surviving Her – Finding Hope Beyond the Pain

I was sexually abused. I was between five and seven years old. I didn't know what was going on or what it was. I just knew a man's hand was in my private area, then it switched to my hands being on his and my mouth was being covered so I wouldn't scream. I was told not to tell anyone; that it was their and my secret game. It went on for a long time – at least that's how it seemed to me. I know it happened more than once because the threats often changed from, it's our secret game, to no one will believe you because I'm family. I don't remember why or how it stopped. You hadn't even noticed, during your random and limited visits, that something was wrong. You should have known, Dad. You were not there – I had no one to run too. I had no one to protect me. You weren't present enough to shield me from the evils of the world.

My teenage years were the worse years of my life. You missed those too. I was looking for love, acceptance, and understanding in a way that a young girl never should. Promiscuity, experimenting with drugs and alcohol, was

Maryann R. Dannert

part of my daily life. Not having anyone to talk to I hung out with my friends' parents because they let me do anything I wanted to do. They had no boundaries. There were many blackout moments, from over-drinking and smoking pot, and sometimes the pot was laced with cocaine. Unfortunately, those behaviors led to me being placed in the custody of the New York State Juvenile Detention System.

God only knows what could have happened to me if I continued on that path. You were not there to look after me, Dad. I didn't feel love at home or that I belonged there. Feeling lost and on my own in juvie, I had no choice but to self-protect. My father refused to safeguard me, so I did it myself the best way I knew how. I learned that before someone had the chance to hurt me, I would hurt them first. I never allowed anyone to get close to me; closeness meant to trust, and I did not trust anyone. Not only did I not trust but I built walls. I built an entire room and it was my safe-haven. If I did not want someone in

Surviving Her — Finding Hope Beyond the Pain

my safe space, they were not going to get in. I became impenetrable. I became unbreakable. I became cold.

Aging out of juvie, I entered the world of adulthood the best way I knew how. I used people just like I was used. In the process, I had my first child.

Still cold, feeling abandoned, and looking for your love, I got married for the first time. I sought refuge in another individual that was supposed to protect and unconditionally love you. Unbeknownst to me, I yet again would be let down. The wall that I was hoping to bring down and the room that I was hoping to permanently unlock became my fortress – again. His question of "what did you do to deserve it" broke my spirit. I ran to the only place that was safe – a bottle of gin. Running from the hurt, I went to where I was safe. Gin had no judgment; boundaries and I couldn't disappoint it! I was damaged goods, and that marriage ended in divorce after four years.

Maryann R. Dannert

As a divorcee, my view of co-parenting changed, and I realized there are always two sides to one story. Although it has taken me a while to arrive at this moment, Dad, I forgive you. I forgive you for not being there. I forgive you for walking out of my life. I forgive you for not sheltering me. You did the best you could.

I love you always & forever,
Your little girl, Maryann

The journey continues, and I have finally realized that life is not a race.

This is life and I will never "arrive." Arriving signifies an end and I am not done living. I used to characterize myself as someone who doesn't easily trust people, and people must earn trust. And while I don't barge into a room like a superhero, with a cape flowing behind me and my hands placed on my hip – announcing myself, I look at trust differently. I trust openly and freely, but cautiously. If an action or conversation sends chills down my spine, I trust that tingly gut feeling. I listen to my internal voice and we have a dialogue. Often, as women, we ignore our gut feeling – as we don't trust ourselves. Trusting ourselves comes with time; we have to do the work to remove the layers of pain. Once you realize and accept one key thing – that is when you will know it is okay and safe to trust yourself, as you've learned to make healthy decisions in your life. Accept and realize *it was not your fault*!

I often wondered what life would look like once I had inner peace. Achieving inner peace can only come from dealing with the pain; I had to move beyond the pain to appreciate and accept hope. We all do what we can with what we have and what we know. I wanted more, and I knew that something was broken, and I wanted and needed a change. I was tired of running. I gave myself permission to seek and accept help – to become vulnerable and to slowly piece back the broken pieces. Counseling did that. While the reason for initially going to counseling was for the sake of my marriage; that allowed the lines of

Maryann R. Dannert

communication with my husband to be opened, allowing me to express myself in a safe and non-judgmental environment. My protective mechanism over the years allowed for others to view me at cold, unapproachable, rude, and mean – but that's not who I am. Not even close.

Today, I have self-confidence and serenity. I'm remarried and this year we will celebrate twelve years of marriage. My three children are healthy and happy. I have accomplished many goals and I continue to inspire, empower and motivate women from coast to coast, to get out of their own way, as they create the life, they've always desired: a life based on their truth and voice. And while I have come to terms with my past and can now talk about it, every day that I wake up, I have to make a conscious decision: continue to play the victim or triumphantly live fearlessly and fabulously!

My hope in sharing my story is that others will permit themselves to be happy. Once you have given yourself permission to be happy, pick up the phone and talk to

Surviving Her — Finding Hope Beyond the Pain

someone. That someone can be a trusted friend, a member of the clergy, or a trained professional. You will feel a shift inside you once you've realized that you deserve happiness. Feel it, embrace it, hold it, and go! Break free from holding yourself hostage because of past wounds. May you find the strength to speak your truth and to courageously be set free! After all, silence is deadly.

In overcoming adversity, I gave myself the go-ahead to become The Fearless Living Coach©. In my coaching; I work with women from all walks of life that feel stuck and in a rut. They may be successful outwardly, but in the inside, they are falling apart – there is a void; they are disillusioned. They are not sure exactly what is missing or how they got to where they are, but they know they are not satisfied with their lives. They desire more but can't figure out what to do next. At some point in your life, you lost yourself – always being there for everybody else, setting your dreams and aspirations on the back burner – forgetting about the most important person…YOU!

Maryann R. Dannert

When women work with me, they walk away with:

• A sense of clarity on who you are and what you desire most in life

• Feel more confident and motivated about your new journey

• Learn how to set realistic goals and positive rewards – while still showing up for others

• Discover negative thought patterns and replace them with positive and uplifting messages

• Have a solid, focused and customized plan that will guide you as you show up and show out in life

• Grow personally and professionally and learn how to live an unapologetic and authentic life – based on your terms

In connection with my coaching, I have co-authored three books, including this very one you are now reading, and I created a workbook titled Journey to Fearless Living©. I

Surviving Her – Finding Hope Beyond the Pain

invite you to act today and do one activity in the workbook – here for free.

In this next activity, I need you to go to that place…the place where you were first hurt…the place where you were violated. If you've never talked to anyone about this, and even if you have, this may be a difficult activity for you. While it may be hard, I urge you to continue – I ask that you keep going! The only way to live and have the life you deserve and desire is to face it, acknowledge it, and accept that it was not your fault!

How old were you? How old are you today?

I need you to write a letter to your younger self. Remember, your younger self was innocent, naïve, trusting, and full of life. Something happened to her – she became broken. Talk to her and tell her all the things you wanted to be told…you're special, it is not your fault, go ahead and cry, go ahead and scream. You now have the

Maryann R. Dannert

power to protect her. Give her lots of hugs and kisses. Hold her tight and do not let her go!

She is you – forever!

I know this activity had to be difficult. After completing it, I hope that this movement was liberating. No matter how hard, we must do the work which will allow us to create the life we deserve and desire. If the pain is not dealt with, it will lead to a tragic end. I would love to hear from you on how you felt and what you got out of the activity.

One of my favorite quotes is one I came across years ago while reading an Oprah magazine: "How can you get to the future when the past is present" – unknown author. The quote literally jumped out at me and has stuck with me ever since. In essence, as human beings, we all seek love, acceptance, and belonging. We all yearn to be part of something that matters. When we enter this world, we enter freely. No pain, no hurts, no violations, no distrust, no opinions, and no manipulations – we are without

Surviving Her – Finding Hope Beyond the Pain

charge. Between those early moments in life, to the current moment today; as you read the words in this book, something happened to you... to us. It could have been one event or many; first and foremost, don't downgrade it. What happened to you – happened! Yet, we cannot live the life we were created to live with the past being present.

I titled my chapter, A Letter to My Dad because deep down I believe my life would have turned out differently had my father been an active participant in it. I don't have a crystal ball, so my assumptions are just that – assumptions. Perhaps my life would have been worse... perhaps I would not have experienced the trauma that I did. But what I do know is that who I am today, is a direct effect of what happened. I also know that the work I have put in and continue to do has transformed me into a woman who is free, happy, fearless, and fabulous! A woman living life on her terms! I no longer resent my past; it is a part of me. It has allowed me to become The Fearless Living Coach© where I seek to inspire, empower and

Maryann R. Dannert

motivate women to move forward in believing that the best is yet to come - as they shape the life they were created to live – Free and Happy!

Facebook @maryanndannert
Instagram @mdannert
Website: www.maryannriveradannert.com
Email: mrdannert@gmail.com

SurvivingHer Author: **Shant'a MILLER**

Shant'a Miller

Shant'a Miller is a mother, entrepreneur, consultant, pioneer and community advocate. She is CEO of P.U.S.H. Professional Consulting, LLC., and Executive Director and founder of the not-for-profit organization "Parents Against Bullying, Inc. (P.A.B.), launched after her family experienced firsthand the traumatic effects of bullying.

Her efforts have garnered recognition and support from individuals and organizations such as: Former First Lady Michelle Obama, U.S. Attorney General, Senator Mark Warner, Mayor McKinley Price, Commonwealth Attorney Howard Gywnn, Attorney General Mark Herring, and many others.

Miller shares her message of healing, restoration, elevation and growth at events throughout the year. She motivates all to be exceedingly great!

The P.U.S.H. Factor

As the bus pulled up to our home and the double doors opened, my usual smile turned into despair as my 6th grade babies exited. One ran frantically towards me crying and shouting while the other limped. Her clothes had been ripped and her hair disheveled- she had been physically assaulted. I later found out her assault lasted for seventeen minutes. Too injured to walk, I carried her in my arms all the way home. For months and now years, this devastating event altered all our lives. Mentally we had to overcome anger and helplessness. Physically, my daughter had to heal under a doctor's care because before the attack, she had been seizure free from epilepsy for almost three years but after the attack she had

Shant'a Miller

a seizure at least five days out of seven. As a mother committed to her children, I felt guilty for not protecting them that day and I needed to make them whole again. I had to speak up for them *and* I had to stop the bullying in my community. This endeavor would challenge and change me forever.

Step by small step, I learned the policies and procedures of the education system. I made valuable contacts, and I never gave up my pursuit of knowledge that was beneficial to everyone connected to me. Against quite a few odds, I learned to maneuver through the bureaucracies and stand firm in my convictions. Through our distress and struggles, I found the voice to tell our story to all who would listen. I was a small business owner with a hair salon at the time and although it cost me customers - daily seizures didn't allow time for hair appointments - I had to do what I had to do to take care of my daughters. Ultimately, I lost my business and my credit was destroyed. So, since I was already down and had nowhere

Surviving Her — Finding Hope Beyond the Pain

to go but up, I took a leap of faith and created Parents' Against Bullying, Virginia (PABVA) - where its aim is to educate and support families involved in bullying incidents and be proactive in their attempts to stop it.

Fast-forward, the twins were doing well in high school and things were lining up for me. I could finally see the light again. True love had finally found me at last. I could find balance in life, love, parenting, and I was still passionate about my non-profit and being its CEO. My calendar was filling up with speaking engagements and workshops. I released my first book and had tours lined up for advocating on the behalf of children and adults. I was in a good place.

Then one day in late February, I kept clearing my throat and feeling like something was wrong. Using the rearview mirror of my car, I opened my mouth and looked inside. One side of my tonsils looked enlarged. I immediately made a U-turn into the urgent care facility that was nearby. After tests and negative results, they referred me

Shant'a Miller

to my family doctor who after three weeks then referred me to an ear, nose and throat physician. As time went on my tonsils continued to grow larger. While I had no pain at this point, my sleep pattern changed. Either I would wake up coughing or choking or awaken because of it. I was scared, and I knew my body and it was telling me, *this is not normal.*

Life had to go on, and it did. During meetings and speaking engagements I had a hard time breathing, but I pressed my way. There were more doctors' visits and many more tests ordered. This went on for over eight weeks with me visiting the Emergency Room on several occasions because it was hard for me to breathe. I could barely eat. I was tired because I couldn't sleep, and my work was suffering as well. Something had to be done. On one visit to the doctor, I begged him to remove my tonsils. He warned me that at my age removing them could be rough on me – it was almost as if he was trying to talk me out of the procedure. But I insisted, and I needed him to match

Surviving Her – Finding Hope Beyond the Pain

my level of urgency because I had an enormous ball in my throat that I knew wasn't supposed to be there. Even at my exams, the staff jumped back and said, "Whoa," when I opened my mouth and they saw the size of it. At that point, I was past being over it. And I would not take no for an answer. I didn't care, I just wanted it done. We scheduled my surgery for May first.

I went to the store the day before my surgery and bought all kinds of popsicles, applesauce, apple juice, pudding, grits and oatmeal. All the things they advise eating after a tonsillectomy. The surgery went well; they biopsied the tissue as a typical procedure and they released me to go home. However, on the second day home I woke up to the most excruciating pain besides childbirth I had ever known. I felt like I had swallowed a box of razors and each time I tried to swallow I was being cut on the inside. My throat was on fire, I was coughing up blood and the bleeding wouldn't stop. I was home alone - the girls were away at school and my fiancé was at work. I didn't know what to do, so I called my mom. With a throat full of blood, my voice couldn't go louder than a whisper. Mom rushed right over, called the doctor and took me in immediately.

The smell and the pain were indescribable. All I could do was moan. From the corner of my eye I saw my mom, and she looked nervous and terrified. As the doctor worked on me, I guess she had reached her threshold and screamed, "Can't you put her to sleep? Please stop. Just take her back to surgery. Please, I can't take what you're doing to my child." Eventually, after cauterizing the incision, the bleeding stopped, and I was sent back home. I have to admit my recovery was tough. Two-weeks later, my fiancé kept telling me he was going with me to my follow-up appointment. I told him, "No, I'll be fine. Every thing's okay now." I am so glad he didn't listen to me.

As soon as my doctor came in he said, "Please don't hate me. The biopsy of your tissue sample revealed you have cancer of the throat." I felt like the air was let out of me.

Surviving Her — Finding Hope Beyond the Pain

All I could think about were my kids. As soon as I heard the word cancer, I thought of dying. The doctor kept talking, but I couldn't hear him. Although I knew the road ahead would be challenging, I was so grateful that I listened to my body and forced the doctor to have the tonsillectomy. I scheduled my second surgery for the next month, June.

While there was full transparency from my medical staff, my home life was the opposite. I hid my diagnosis from my twins. Their high school graduation was coming up, and I wanted them to graduate with happy hearts and to be excited about their next steps. College awaited them. I wanted to have everything perfect so no one would be worried about me, so I kept postponing and pushing the surgery date further and further away. It was like I was stuck and couldn't move forward. Petrified of what could happen. I didn't tell anyone that I was diagnosed with head and neck cancer. I did not stop my work with PABVA, even though I was suffering physically. The children and their parents relied on me at a moment's notice for advice and feedback and needed me to be at my best. So, I kept pushing and praying, which I've learned most of the time the two go hand in hand. I put off my surgery so many times that I had to sign a medical release form. They did not want to be responsible if something bad happened to me – and I understood their position. I was just trying to keep my life as normal as possible for as long as I could.

August rolled around and my fiancé took me to the hospital at five in the morning. He kissed me on my forehead as tears ran down my face, not knowing what was next. After seven hours I woke up in Intensive Care Unit (ICU) very groggy to see the shadow of him sitting in a chair in the corner of my room. I had a feeding tube down my nose. Two tubes running out of my neck and a cut from behind my ear to the middle of my throat. I had two cuts on the top of my shoulder blade. But he didn't leave my side. Three days later, I was still in the ICU and my

Surviving Her — Finding Hope Beyond the Pain

doctor walked in and gave the greatest news ever... I was cancer free. No radiation needed. No chemo needed.

Look at God! My scars aren't ugly — they are truly my testimony. Every day when I look in the mirror and touch them, see them and they give me hope. I am even stronger today than yesterday. My goals and agenda have not changed. In fact, I am more rejuvenated than ever. I have been blessed with more time and I will not waste it. I am reminded that I pushed through. To push means to move forward using force to get past something or someone. And as CEO for P.U.S.H. Professional Consulting, LLC. that is my motto and what I live by. P.U.S.H. (Patience, Understanding, and the Stability to Handle My Business)

I always say, "everyone has a story, but it is what you do with yours that makes a difference." I chose to share mine. A story of what it really means to be unstoppable. I stopped asking myself *why me* and instead said, *why not me?* I have learned as I have healed, when we share our experiences with each other, maybe we can even save someone's life. If I can help someone, anyone, make it through the day or empower someone to reach their next goal and achieve something that fills their heart with good, then I have accomplished a great thing.

My family and I have become a closer family unit because we've learned not to take life for granted. My oldest daughter has pursued higher education while being a mom, and the twins are in culinary school pushing themselves to the next level. My bonus kids and Derek and I are doing well. I am more in love with Derek than I have ever been. My life is peaceful, and we are making it through prayer and works. I am a living, walking and talking testimonial. I P.U.S.H. and live by God's grace and his mercy. I hope my story serves as a reminder for you to do the same.

"Trust in the Lord with all your heart and lean not onto your own understanding. In all your ways acknowledge Him and He shall direct your path."

Surviving Her — Finding Hope Beyond the Pain

— Proverbs 3:5-6

My biggest dream in life is to leave a legacy for my children and grandchildren that no man can rewrite and to lead by example under the direction of God.

Always remember: You are a Star: Successful and Smart, Terrific and Talented, Amazing and Awesome and Refuse to be put down.

Did you know...

On the website www.stopbullying.gov, it states that youth between the ages of 12-18 are bullied at school. Another national statistic regarding bullying states that approximately 30% of young people admit to bullying 57% of the time, but when bystanders get involved, the bully stops within 10 seconds (Facts About Bullying 2017).

PABVA is always here to assist and guide in identifying bullying, reporting the issues, creating action plans and

Shant'a Miller

finding solutions if your child is being bullied or is the bully. Through community support the mission of PABVA has grown into many positive outreach opportunities such as school tours, youth marches, Stand Your Ground 4 Peace step shows and creating No Bully Zones with visible PABVA signs with a large green hand indicating entrance into a #NoBullyZone. Bullying is a real epidemic, and it is time to end it worldwide.

Let's P.U.S.H: A Guide to Combat Bullying – is a book that I authored in which readers will learn more of my personal journey and the specifics of the PABVA movement. The book goes into more detail regarding the bullying incident my daughter endured. It provides tips and steps on what to do about bullying issues. It is available for purchase online at Amazon and Barnes & Noble.

Keep in touch with us and find updates for PABVA at www.pabva.com and to donate to our cause.

Surviving Her – Finding Hope Beyond the Pain

Facebook @ShantaNicole
Instagram @Shantanicole_
Email: shanta.miller2013@gmail.com

Surviving Her ANTHOLOGY

Finding Hope Beyond the Pain

SurvivingHer Author: *Natalie PURDIE*

Natalie Purdie

Was a victim of a violent attack by her boyfriend as a teenager. The person who attacked her received a lenient sentence with no time in jail. Years later Natalie was a surprise witness against the same person. This would be the beginning of Natalie finally breaking her silence and being able to do what she has always desired to do, "Speak Up and Speak Out!"

Natalie is a board member and volunteer with My Help My Hope, Inc., and Promise Place.

Natalie is currently helping many victims of domestic violence to become survivors. She works behind the scenes with friends and families of victims and survivors. Her goal is to continue to travel all over the world to tell her story to help others by raising awareness and prevention. She wants to teach your youth and speak at your conference.

WARNING: The following story may be considered graphic to some readers, and names have been changed to protect their privacy.

Surviving Another Trial

Ms. Purdie, my name is Beth and I'm an investigator for the Commonwealth of Virginia. Is there somewhere you and I can talk in private?" I got up from my desk at work and lead the way into a private room. Our meeting that day changed my life.

Beth was working on an open case of the brutal attack of a woman, and the person accused of doing it was the same person who viciously stabbed me over 20 years ago. The mere sound of his name sent so many emotions through me all at once. It was like a scary movie when the frightening part approaches as the monster lurks closer. Instantly a release of tears flowed. Beth remained quiet,

Natalie Purdie

but I could tell she realized that not only was I the person she was looking for, but perhaps there was more to my story.

Composed as much as I could be, the investigator asked if she could record our conversation, but once I told my complete story, she forgot all about taping me. The details shocked her; It was 1986, and I was 18 years old. My boyfriend of five months with a pair of scissors I had just used to cut out my senior portraits with, stabbed me in my face, nose, chin, lips, behind my ear, hands, arms, upper torso, and legs. Because I wanted to break up with him, I was left in a pool of blood as he ran out of my grandparent's home. Left to deal with the aftermath, I had bleeding on the brain and a skull fracture. I had post-traumatic seizures. I also had to re-learn how to talk, walk, and to read. Beth was mortified when she read in a file how the charges of attempted murder were dropped to a misdemeanor (unlawful wounding). And while they sentenced him – he served no jail time. Beth slid her chair closer to me as she informed me that since my attack, he had attacked other women and like my situation, he had gotten away with it. The specific case she was investigating he purposely rear-ended his girlfriend's car. He walked to her driver's side window and kept hitting her. He then tried to gouge out her left eye. When that didn't work, he bit off a chunk of her cheek and spat it on the ground. All for again, she wanted to get out of the relationship. Beth said none of the past victims would testify against him. Hearing there were other victims, and that nothing had stopped him, made me cringe. If they had only convicted him when he attacked me or gotten him help, maybe those attacks would have been prevented. No matter how many if's I thought of, none of them changed how my heart ached. I always hoped I was his only victim and that since he got away with it, he'd learn his lesson and would never hurt another like he had me. The last time I went to trial, nothing went in my favor. So, when I was told he got away with other attacks, it felt like he had stabbed me thirty times all over again. I knew that I had to help in any way

Natalie Purdie

that I could to try to prevent further attacks from happening to another woman. Beth asked me to testify again, and I agreed. As the investigator exited, I told her that it would be at least a year before we went to trial. My attacker used every delay tactic he could to delay our trial date. He hoped that I'd get tired and give up. As I walked back to my desk, I tried to prepare myself to face him again. I couldn't think of any preparation except to pray and be still. I knew I couldn't share the news with anyone.

Weeks turned into months, and months turned into over a year for the trial. The entire time was torture for me. Each time I thought it was time for me to go to court, I received a call saying the case was being continued. It devastated me. I felt defeated, cheated, angry, and scared. I felt pain for the victim. Although I didn't know her, I knew how she was feeling. Was he going to be released again with a slap on the wrist? I prayed that justice would be served. I prayed for the victim's healing. I prayed for my own healing because I felt like I was reliving a

Surviving Her — Finding Hope Beyond the Pain

nightmare all over again and keeping the biggest secret of my life. I didn't share it with anyone for several reasons. My grandfather had just passed away, and I didn't want my family to be worried. I also couldn't take everyone asking questions because I knew it would lead to anxiety, fear, stress, and I wouldn't be able to function or focus. Last but not least, I couldn't tell a soul because I would testify as a surprise witness for the Prosecuting Attorney.

September 10, 2012. "I need everyone to remain calm and stay quiet. We don't have that much time for me to explain everything to you. Just know when I come into the courtroom I will be testifying." I had just told some of my family that I had to go to court, and they wanted to come along.

Arriving at the courthouse, all my thoughts shifted to the victim. The witness protection advocate told me she was not coming to court - at all. While I get it – she probably didn't want the entire courtroom staring at her. She had eye damage, reconstructive surgery, and had permanent

Natalie Purdie

facial scarring from the attack. I know a big reason she didn't come to court was out of fear; fear that he may not receive any actual prison time; fear that when he looked at her, he took pride in the scars he gave her. But there were so many things I wanted to say to her face-to-face. Her scars wouldn't have scared me – I have them too. If she didn't want to talk, I was okay with that as well, but I wanted to let her know that she would eventually heal one day. I also wanted to apologize for our judicial system that failed me, which I believe lead to her becoming a victim.

The courtroom was extremely quiet when I walked in and there were a lot of deputies with guns – which made me feel a little better, especially when I entered the witness stand. I raised my right hand and said, "I do solemnly and sincerely and truly declare and affirm that the evidence I shall give shall be the truth, the whole truth, and nothing but the truth. ... I promise before Almighty God that the evidence which I shall give shall be the truth, the whole truth, and nothing but the truth." I meant every word. As

Surviving Her – Finding Hope Beyond the Pain

soon as I sat down, I tried to take in everything, who was in the courtroom, the looks on their faces, his parents, his friends, his lawyer, him. They looked serious but not worried. As far as they were concerned, he was going home like he always did.

Confident, I recalled the attack and how it affected my life, my future, and my health. The entire time I spoke, he would not look at me. I guess I was a tangible reminder of something he had done 25 years ago and wanted to forget - especially at that moment. While I was testifying a woman got up and left the room. Her face had a look of shock. Immediately after I finished, I exited the stand, walked past him, and sat within the safety and comfort of my family. As the closing arguments began both attorneys were very prompt and precise with their delivery. The verdict judgment was swift as the judge's voice was not loud when he sentenced him to 35 years in prison - nearly twice the maximum amount. None of the time was suspended, which will have him in jail for the rest of his

Natalie Purdie

life. Someone screamed in anguish. I was in shock as everyone in the courtroom was. I was then whisked away into a room to keep me safe from the crowd.

While I was waiting in the room, my family entered, and they were still so disturbed to hear everything that was said in the courtroom. They were just as upset as they were when it first happened. My brothers wanted to protect me and retaliate, but I calmed them down as much as I could.

A newspaper reporter approached me and asked for an interview. Although I was still overwhelmed with so many emotions, I agreed because I wanted people to know what justice looked like even though it wasn't my case.

A few hours later, I had an interview with a local news channel. It differed from the newspaper because it would allow people to look, listen, and even recognize me. The hardest decision was telling my story in detail (outside of a courtroom) for all to know, but I knew the only way to really help others would be to tell what happened to me.

SurvivingHer — Finding Hope Beyond the Pain

It wasn't until afterward would I know the extreme effects and benefits that come with releasing the pain. I healed each time I told my story. Not only that, I learned the lesson that is tied to my purpose and the assignment, my mission. God didn't just save me for himself but to help others, to raise awareness, educate, and to eradicate violence. I am SurvivingHer.

Now I talk to anyone who will listen and even those who don't. I am a voice for the voiceless. I am the survivor's voice. If you had a stroke and it has temporarily paralyzed, you keep striving to regain the strength to walk and talk. I didn't have a speech impairment, but I have daily challenges and I am here to face them. Everyone has their own experience and impact on how it affects them. Our pain and healing may be different and some similar, but I can relate, inspire, encourage, listen, motivate, and offer resources. I can't give up because then I can't be here to speak. Nobody can tell your story better than you. We are all here for a purpose and if you give up, you may never

Natalie Purdie

know what the purpose is! I now know that being an advocate and speaker, this is My Purpose and I also know that there is more to my story. You can't be a survivor if you didn't fight against whatever it was. So even if you don't feel you are strong, if you survived, you are. Keep a journal and it not only will help you recall your feelings it will also help you see where you were and how you are not there anymore. Give yourself a pat on the back, applaud yourself, seek a help group for a cause that may have affected you or a family member, become a mentor, volunteer, or donate to a foundation. Each one of us can help, hope, and heal to make a difference.

Today I advocate for *all* children, women, and men who are victims of domestic violence. I am here to raise prevention and awareness about domestic violence, child abuse, sexual assault, suicide, depression. We must educate ourselves to stop the violence. Prevention saves lives, money, and minimizes complications. Early intervention is the next best thing. Studies show that violence doesn't

Surviving Her — Finding Hope Beyond the Pain

just lead to homicides but depression, drugs, suicide, poverty, and child abuse to name a few. I am here to help people to know what to do and know about seeking justice, protection, and getting resources. When faced with a tragedy people don't know what to do especially because you don't think that it will happen to you or someone in your family. I try to help families because I know they may experience what my family felt, and it is hard to know what to do. I would not want anyone to endure a tragedy, unfortunately that is not the structure of the world we now live in. Therefore, my biggest hope is that someone will remember something that I said that will help them. Sometimes I think about what the doctors said, and then I think of all the things I have overcome. Sometimes I wonder if nobody wants to hear my story again, or maybe I should give up. Just when I am thinking about giving up, I receive a call or email from someone reaching out to me for help. Or, someone will reach out to me to say they just saw one of the television shows about my story and it helped them. So often it is the confirmation that I need to help me know that I am making a difference and that it is still not about me. I've got a testimony. God wanted me to tell it, but he wanted to make sure that the right people were listening and that I was ready mentally and physically. My scripture is Genesis 50:20 "What was meant for evil, God uses for good." I am ready to live my dream, desire, and destiny to travel all around the world for people to hear my voice because I have so much to talk about it. Other people have just as much to talk about and information that will help me grow as an individual, and an advocate. I am not just a survivor, I thrive. Let's talk about it. No person, place, audience, or topic is too small. When I speak, I feel rejuvenated, restored, and it is therapeutic. I am available for your audience whether it is a conference, company training, youth organization, special event, or function.

Surviving Her – Finding Hope Beyond the Pain

Facebook: @nataliepurdiesv
Instagram: @survivors_voice
Linkedin: @natalie-purdie.
Email: nataliepurdie@yahoo.com

Surviving Her ANTHOLOGY
Finding Hope Beyond the Pain

SurvivingHer Author: Stacey D.M. SHAW

Stacey D. M. Shaw

Is an author, certified coach, speaker, radio host, business owner, and the founder of a non-profit organization, Destined to Be Free, a domestic violence awareness organization.

Stacey is a contributing author for "My Son" (12/20) and is writing her next book "The Day that I Broke Free." She is the founder of BraNelle, Inc. a real estate consulting and operations company, the VP and Chief Admin. Officer for Elevation Global Media Group. Stacey received coaching certifications in Christian Biblical Life and Soul-Care, and is a licensed real estate sales associate.

Her greatest joy is serving the Lord, motherhood, exploring nature and the beach, and dancing to music while being silly and fun-loving.

You Broke Me. You Shattered Me. But You Never Destroyed Me

It was a bright and beautiful morning and the children had begun their summer vacation, which I had all planned out. We were going to Jamaica to spend the next five weeks with my husband, my baby, the love of my life. Tony and I met when I was 24 years old. We dated for two years, was married for eighteen of which we were separated for seven years. Tony is a hardworking man and really good with words - a charmer with the smile to match. The kids and I were so excited to see him because we hadn't seen him for six months. I couldn't wait for the moment when I could run into his arms and feel them snuggly around me. Soon we'd all be together – one big happy family. That morning we woke up early and headed

Stacey D.M. Shaw

to Orlando International Airport to take a flight to Kingston, Jamaica. As the plane landed at Norman Manley International Airport, I started having butterflies like a kid in a candy store. When he saw me, we kissed, and he hugged the children then drove to his mom's house where he was living. That night we had a wonderful night of passion between us. The following day, I cleaned and organized his room more than I had done on my previous visits. I wanted to give it my wife's touch and my antenna's, my womanly intuition, was stirring. So, while cleaning, I opened his dresser drawer and found two envelopes. One was sealed with a woman's name on it and the other was an opened plain white envelope. Inside the envelope was a written agreement between my husband and this lady in which he had given her J$140,000 (US $1,500.00) The blood inside my entire body boiled because here I was back in the states, not working and with the kids and he's here on an exotic island giving away our money. My cleaning turned into a full-on search. I read everything there was. I went through bags, drawers,

Surviving Her — Finding Hope Beyond the Pain

closets, and his clothes pockets. I found condoms in his laptop bag. I then opened his laptop and found messages where he emailed this woman, telling her how much he was thinking of her. Everything in my world paused as my heart sunk and the tears flowed down my cheeks. My fears of him cheating had hit me straight in the face. Who is this b----? My head spun as fast as the question began. Who in the hell was this woman, and what did she have that I didn't?

Feeling many emotions but betrayal was at the top of the list, I stomped into my mother-in-law's room and told her all that I had found. Even with proof, however, she defended him anyway. Oh, the pain that pierced through my heart, and the knots in my stomach that made me nauseous. That evening when he walked into his bedroom, I confronted him about all that I had found. His glib response was basically he worked, it was his money, and he didn't need my permission for anything. When I asked about the condoms, he sucked his teeth and walked into the bathroom. I sat and waited for an answer, but I was shocked at his response.

"My father told my mom whenever she searched his things, it was her fault if she found something. I guess you're just like her!"

I was so damn naïve. I accepted what he said, even though I knew deep down what he said made no sense. We continued to argue back and forth. My tears kept falling, and he had no remorse. That night, I still wanted to be intimate with him because Tony had a way of drawing me into his web. We had sex- it was cold and distant. I had no self-esteem; my entire marriage was about pleasing my husband despite the hurt and pain I endured.

The next morning, he woke up like nothing ever happened – like he wasn't cheating and spending all our money. As he walked out of the door, I noticed he wasn't wearing his wedding band. The next thing that bugged the crap out of me was that he wouldn't wear his wedding band. I assumed he stopped wearing his ring because he didn't want anyone to know he was married and had children. But I needed to know, so I asked, "where is your wedding band?" He told me that it was in his drawer as he couldn't wear it because when he goes out of the house he flirts, and the wedding band would prevent him from speaking to ladies. He couldn't help it if women throw themselves at him and if one of them drops their pants in front of him, he'd just have to do what he had to do. He also told me that I should never let him have to choose between me and his lady friend.

Was he serious? I hate to break it to you dude, but you are married, how dare you?

I cried, and that's all I could do. My husband was with other women and he flaunted it in my face and I still stayed with him. I wanted to hold on to my marriage – my family. Honestly, I thought he was the only man that would ever love me – that would ever see me. Again, I felt like I had no other options. He was my idol. I gave up

Stacey D.M. Shaw

everyone and everything for him. I took his verbal abuse for six more years until I had no more to give. I returned to Jamaica one more time after that visit and never returned.

One day through casual conversation with my son in the living room, he told me that when we lived with Tony in the states; he hated me because I never protected him. Tony was not my son's biological father, and he'd beat my son when I was not at home. He had even planned to run away because the abuse was so severe and felt as if I would choose Tony over him. This confession was my light bulb moment. I looked at the pain in my baby's eyes and I fell to my knees and apologized to him. When I stood to my feet, there was something about me that had changed. I was no longer a pawn – I felt strengthened on the inside. I made the motion of washing my hands. My son's physical abuse was where I drew the line. That was the day I decided to proceed with my divorce. I was done!

Surviving Her – Finding Hope Beyond the Pain

The experiences endured throughout my life have changed me in positive ways and allowed me to open not only my eyes but my heart, as well as accepting that my soul needed healing. I know I still have a long way to go in the healing process, however, despite it all I am grateful to God for never leaving and never giving up on me. I realized that I hadn't experienced life to the extent others around me had. I only existed and had no clue about many things because I was never taught or hadn't experienced them. It is now time for Stacey to live, time for me to experience life the way God intended for me. Time for Stacey to be filled with peace, joy, happiness, and true genuine love.

Admitting that I needed healing and taking the necessary steps helped me to implement and make drastic changes. I journal'd and meditated on specific scriptures or quotes that aided me in getting through each day. I created a workbook and a journal which included a few of the steps below which I implemented in my life as I walked out my healing:

Stacey D.M. Shaw

- Realizing how beautiful I am and that I needed to adjust how I dressed and to walk with confidence.

- Understanding that I couldn't change on my own. I needed a spiritual coach that would understand; someone who would guide me in fulfilling my calling.

- I need a counselor because there was so much pain that I needed to release.

- Began valuing money and working on my credit and net worth.

- Setting boundaries.

- Started working on my health to eliminate health issues.

- Initiated a multigenerational plan to leave a legacy for my children and grandchildren.

- Being a servant to those less fortunate.

- I sought God and his Kingdom because I didn't know who Stacey was and who she wanted to become. I learned

Surviving Her – Finding Hope Beyond the Pain

how to shed my false persona and destroy the identity crisis I had developed over the years.

At this point in my life, I am so in love with God and I am finding my peace. I am now working on what I was born to do, and I refuse to look back. I started a domestic violence awareness organization, and I recently became certified as a soul care practitioner (a coach who assists in healing). I am now equipped with the knowledge to work with survivors and those who have experienced trauma. I also want to provide affordable housing to survivors, giving them a place to call home, so at the end of 2019 I became a Maryland real estate associate–prayerfully they will either start their own business or assist them in returning to corporate America.

There were so many red flags and opportunities to walk away in all my situations, but I chose not to acknowledge what they were. So, my heart aches for anyone who has experienced any form of trauma in their lives. And no trauma is greater than the other because the impact on

Stacey D.M. Shaw

each person is different. My specific pain may not be yours, but that doesn't mean your pain is less. I've learned the hard lesson that if the pain is not released, and the real me stays buried, I'd forever be bound. And God doesn't want that for me or you! We want you to live the life you're created to live and accomplish all that you have dreamed about. My best advice is to know who you are; know whose you are and who stands and walks with you. There is nothing in this world that you cannot do or overcome.

Below is a list of helpful things to help aid you in finding the real you:

1. Find a park or a gym. Create a schedule and be as consistent as possible with either walking/running or exercising. Having a quiet place to work out or just walk and enjoy nature allows you to experience peace and help you think clearly.

Surviving Her — Finding Hope Beyond the Pain

2. Write. Writing is therapy. Don't worry about how or what you are writing or worry about formatting. Just write. There will be tears, but I promise you, you will begin to feel lighter.

3. Serve anywhere you can. It could be monthly, quarterly, but just serve. By serving it will give you clarity, and it just may assist you in walking straight into your true calling.

4. Surround yourself with genuine friends who will stand with you and guide you; You will need non-judgmental friends and family around you.

5. Seek a therapist when you are ready and seek a coach. A coach who is understanding and willing to guide and assist you. Locate a mentor as well.

6. Read as much as you can. Find your hobbies.

7. Realize that you are unique and wonderfully made and you have a massive assignment that only you can do.

Stacey D.M. Shaw

Words are powerful, find specific words to speak over yourself daily.

8. Seek the Kingdom of God, *very important*

9. Love yourself. Enjoy You, Laugh, and Have Fun!

Two scriptures that I stand on...

"Then said the Lord unto me, Thou hast well seen for I will hasten my word to perform it." Jeremiah 1:12

"Ye have not chosen me, but I have chosen you, and ordained you, that ye should go and bring forth fruit, and that your fruit should remain: that whatsoever ye shall ask of the Father in my name, he may give it to you." John 15:16

My biggest desire for everyone is to live a life of peace and joy in the Kingdom, healed and to know their true identity and walk in their calling. Life is about living and walking in total freedom. Live your life, Enjoy Your Life and Be Free. I was broken, I was shattered, but I was never

Surviving Her — Finding Hope Beyond the Pain

destroyed; My brokenness became my blessing and I am now embracing my rebirth.

Website: www.staceydmshaw.com
Facebook, Twitter: @staceydmshaw
Instagram and Linkedin: @staceydmshaw
Email:Stacey@staceydmshaw.com

*Dear Stephanie, (cuz)
Thank you so much for the support! I greatly appreciate it! Sincerely,
Lia Heather*

Surviving Her ANTHOLOGY

Finding Hope Beyond the Pain

SurvivingHer Author: *Kiana L. STALLWORTH*

Kiana L. Stallworth

Coach, author and entrepreneur, Kiana's greatest fulfillment doesn't come from awards or accolades, but from empowering others to walk in their purpose. As a survivor of sexual abuse, her straight-talk approach allows her to encourage people to push past their pain and soar.

With a B.S degree in Public Administration from Central Michigan University, Kiana partners with non-profit organizations, including the Stewart Lula Belle Center, Women of Color STEM Conference, Children's Hospital of Michigan and Habitat for Humanity.

Kiana had the honor of being a featured co-author in her first anthology, *Coach My Life* with her chapter entitled, *Are you F.R.E.E. (Finally Ready to Emotionally Evolve)?* Kiana is releasing a solo book project soon. Whether she's speaking at a women's empowerment event, or coaching women one-on-one, she is committed to transforming the world, one life at a time.

Turning Pain Into Success

I didn't choose to become a victim, nor did I choose the path my life started on.

Every girl wants to believe the very best about their father, I know I did. My dad was the cool one in the neighborhood. He was always happy, dancing and the life of the party. I didn't think he could do any wrong. Innocently, we often played – him biting and pinching me on my behind. I was a quiet and meek child. When it came to my father, I kind of accepted a little bit of everything – I didn't know any better and I loved him. I believed everything he told me was bond. But that bond eroded when, from the period between kindergarten and middle school, my biological dad sexually and mentally abused me. Cunning, the abuse didn't start until after my mother left for work. That's when he would force me out of my sleep and into their bedroom and do all types of sexual acts on me. The stench of his alcohol and cigarette breath always filled the air. He told me that if I told anyone what he was doing to me that he would go to jail and eventually, we both will go to jail. I believed him.

I was excited to begin my eighth-grade school year. It was a pivotal year because I was looking forward to high school. We had so many field trips, I was in the band and our teachers had planned all kinds of 8th-grade activities for us up until graduation. I was dating and talking on the phone to guys. I was a typical teenager. However, this year, my father became overly strict and controlling.

I can recall a day when he was drunk and had asked me to get in the bed with him. I was old enough to understand what he wanted. I refused, but it hadn't been the first time I had done so. There were other times before where he would go back downstairs, and I thought he finally

Surviving Her — Finding Hope Beyond the Pain

understood that I did not want to be abused anymore. But this time, when I fell back to sleep, there was another tap on my shoulder. As I tiredly walked towards his room, I remember saying to myself, this is it, I can't take it no more! I undressed and just laid there as he had his way with me. His touch made my stomach nausea, I had to vomit. I felt trapped. As sexual intercourse took its course, I thought about what was being taken away from me. I thought, "why do you keep doing this?" When it was over, I left the room feeling disgusted because it just wasn't right.

My father approached me on many occasions to have sex with him. Each time I told him, "no," and I did not give in. My refusal made him more aggressive and controlling. I could no longer have male friends or talk on the phone. The time I was spending over a friend's house was limited. Sometimes I would threaten him that I would tell my mom. On one occasion, I went to call my mom, and he pulled the plug right out of the wall. His eyes were

Kiana L. Stallworth

bloodshot and glossy as if something had jumped in his body and taken over. It was scary. I couldn't understand what was happening. It was like he was an unfamiliar person. He had been drinking, of course, but this behavior still was off. My dad got angry, and cursed, "You not telling her a muthaf------ thing. I ran upstairs where my sister was. I closed the door, and he didn't come after me... this time.

After that confrontation, I feared daily what could happen next. I was tired of living in fear and being controlled by him. I could no longer go on with things the way they were. This is what ultimately led me to want to confide in my mom. But I knew I had to figure out a way and when it would be a good time to tell. It took a couple of days because I went back and forth and practiced in my head what I would say. Would my mom believe me, how will the family react, and will my truth break up our family?

One evening, Mom was in the kitchen cooking and my dad had gone out somewhere. I said, "Ma, daddy is

Surviving Her — Finding Hope Beyond the Pain

touching me, and I don't like it but every time I tell him no he gets mad." Ma stopped cooking and asked me, "What do you mean touching you?" The moment I opened my mouth and poured out my truth, it was at that moment, I felt instant relief. The pain and embarrassment, the feeling bad for my mom, and worry were finally off my shoulders. My mom did the right thing and took me immediately to the police station to file a report and we did not go back to that house - until my father went to jail. We went through the process of my parents divorcing, but there was never really a period of counseling and healing for us. It was like what happened happened, and then everyone just moved on the best way they could – including me. People around us knew what happened, but the rippling effects it caused, no one had a clue. I kept it to myself, tried to ignore it, and brushed it off as I'm good. Honestly, at 14 years old, I didn't realize I was even going through trauma.

Kiana L. Stallworth

As I morphed from my late teens to a young adult, I noticed that I was timid as times. I needed the approval of others, and when I communicated, I sometimes sounded like I wasn't sure of myself. This made me put other's needs before my own. I was soft-spoken and when someone complimented me, I always downplayed it. I also went through a period of feeling bad for my dad because he couldn't find a job because of his criminal record. Thinking that if we didn't go to the authorities and handled this within the family, he would not have a record with sexual abuse on it. Throughout the years until he died, the best way to describe our relationship was we were cordial. I still loved him, but he had no father privileges - meaning he had no say-so over my life and my decisions.

By the time I was in my mid-thirties, I had suffered multiple panic attacks. At times I was unhappy, emotionally drained, and I felt stuck and alone. I moved from relationship to relationship so that I wouldn't feel any void in between. I needed to be loved all the time. I

Surviving Her — Finding Hope Beyond the Pain

was searching for love from any man because I didn't experience it from my father. But I had major trust issues. And when my relationships would end, I went through self-blame, and my self-confidence plummeted. I knew there was much more to life than the path I was on. I couldn't understand why I was failing in my relationships, why my marriage didn't last long, why it was taking so long for me to accomplish things, what was my purpose in life and why was God allowing me to still be here on earth, was questions I was asking myself. I felt like I was just existing but not living life to its full potential. My sons were growing up right before my eyes, so I knew I needed to work on my psychological health. I thought to myself if I'm weak and unstable, that would influence them and my oldest was already acting out in school and was labeled as having ADHD. It wasn't until I started seeking help with a counselor/Christian coach, that I realized that some underlining issues stem from my childhood of being sexually abused by my father. I decided to take control over my life and in that; I had to dig down into the root of where some of these issues stem from.

I pulled back important layers of my life that hindered me from succeeding in three steps.

Step 1: I forgave my father. It was a process. It wasn't easy, but I did it. I had the willingness to change, grow, and evolve. I chose to free myself from the anger, hurt, and bitterness that I had bottled up inside me. I felt that if I continued to let what he did to me affect my daily life, then I was still giving him too much power over me. But choosing to forgive him, I gave myself the greatest gift - a sense of peace. Also, I no longer wanted to harbor any more negative feelings about what happened. Because operating in unforgiveness left me stressed and stress kills. It wasn't any good for my health to be anxious about trying to figure out why he wronged me. The real benefit I gained was when I let go. At the end of the day, I'm not perfect and one day I will need someone to forgive me. I didn't forgive my father for him; I did it for me.

Second, I received the therapy I needed to help peel back the layers that delayed my growth. I began to understand how my trauma influenced my intimate relationships and marriage. I was made aware of the relation between how I attracted certain men. I used defense mechanisms whenever I felt disrespected, and my verbal communication was not healthy at all. I felt the need to stand up for myself and to prove that I would not let anyone mistreat me like my dad treated my mom. I learned the differences between being assertive and aggressive. I worked on techniques to help my anxiety that included meditating, reading, and reciting affirmations. These things helped me believe in myself again. I started journaling and writing down what made me happy. I listed all the things that I had accomplished and the things I was afraid to conquer. I picked one task a week to do, and when I accomplished it my self-esteem was boosted tremendously. One of my issues was not having enough time to accomplish goals with my 9-5 consuming all my time. However, that changed when I read a book called

Kiana L. Stallworth

Miracle Morning by Hal Elrod. It's a great book that gave me tips on how to form habits that helped me to reach my full potential by showing me how to make use of the time I didn't normally use.

Once I felt healed emotionally, the third and last step was acquired as a Life Coach and working towards accomplishing goals that I had set for myself. It seemed like every goal I had there were speed bumps in the road, but I kept going no matter what. I finished school and received my degree in Public Administration. My thinking shifted, and I learned how to turn negatives into positives. Like when I moved back into my mom's house. I was able to rent my house out, pay off my debt, and then purchase a new home. My life is not about giving up but finding alternative routes to meet my goals.

One goal I pushed to the side was writing a book about my story. Because deep down inside, I've always wanted to motivate and encourage other women like me – a victim of sexual abuse. I know I am here to serve a purpose and I

Surviving Her — Finding Hope Beyond the Pain

have a desire to help people. The greatest joy in the world is to impact humanity. God saved me and I want to pay it forward. I learned that sometimes God chooses certain people to go through various situations in life for a reason. My greatest joy is helping women and men find their purpose and becoming unstuck from whatever may hold them in bondage. One scripture that resonates with me is Jeremiah 29:11 "For I know the plans I have for you, declares the Lord, plans for welfare and not for evil, to give you a future and a hope." With faith, hope, love, and a plan, I am unstoppable.

Right now, I am living life to the fullest. I am blessed, and I thank God for continuing to bless me. My oldest is 21 and has just graduated from trade school and my youngest is 14. Both are my world. I started my coaching business, Coach Me to Freedom, where I help women and men break free mentally and physically because of their past trauma. My goal is to bring clarity to areas of confusion and help them live life to the fullest.

Kiana L. Stallworth

One of my favorite scriptures is "I can do all things through Christ which strengthened me." Philippians 4:13. Another one is 1 Thessalonians 5:11 "Therefore encourage one another and build one another up, just as you are doing."

My biggest hope for humanity is for anyone that has experienced sexual abuse trauma to take that experience and turn it into a positive outcome. Once we have healed, we must reach out and give back. We were put on this earth to serve a purpose. This could help the next victim, becoming an advocate for what we have overcome and fighting to regain peace and sanity. We never know who we are inspiring or motivating with our story.

Also, my biggest hope for humanity is that since sexual abuse and assault has now come to the forefront, where people are being more vocal regarding reporting abuse and confronting their abuser, that the support will continue so people will not be afraid to come forward and abusers can be held accountable.

Surviving Her – Finding Hope Beyond the Pain

Facebook @CoachmetoFreedom
Instagram @Coachkee_
Website: www.traumacoachkiana.com
Email: kianastallworth@gmail.com

Surviving Her ANTHOLOGY
Finding Hope Beyond the Pain

SurvivingHer Author: *Chierda* WASHINGTON

Chiezda Washington

Holistic Life Coach and Health Ambassador. Affectionately called "Energy on Fire," this powerhouse drafted into her purpose, fully embraced becoming a Holistic Life Coach after having stood by as her mother battled a chronic illness. A native Washingtonian, she is passionate about educating, empowering and equipping individuals and families on the subjects that matter most: Health and Finances!

Founder of Health Ambassadors Ltd, one of her greatest attributes is the ability to support others becoming their best selves. When she is not championing for change in the health industry, she's enjoying books on leadership and self-development.

I Love You but I Love Me More

Love is patient, is kind, does not envy, does not boast, is not proud, does not dishonor others, is not self-seeking, is not easily angered, keeps no records of wrongs, does not delight in evil, rejoices with the truth, always protects, always trusts, always hopes, always perseveres and NEVER FAILS."1 Corinthians 13:4-8

LOVE…what a word to believe in and believed in it I did. I was 18 years old when I met the father of my children. It was fall and I was fresh out of high school, selling life insurance. This morning, I'd gotten up, put on my favorite navy-blue skirt suit, and headed out of the door. I had on my black pumps and my favorite hairstyle, a blunt bob with bangs. David and I, my insurance associate,

Chiezda Washington

headed to the U.S. Department of State as one of our stops for the day to seek new clients for our custom federal government insurance policy. There we were, in the halls of the state department, and he walked by. Dressed to the nines, he wore blue jeans, a blue jean shirt, a brown suede belt, and matching brown suede loafers. He was 6'3 inches tall and light-skinned, well-groomed, and smelled absolutely delicious.

David said, "Just walk up to him and speak and see what happens." Well, I did, and our first introduction turned into a lunch meeting that lasted the rest of the day. For the next several weeks, Ronald (8 years my senior) and I courted one another, and we became serious, quick. He and I also became parents just as fast as our first daughter was born 1 year after we met. We were on a roller coaster and I had belted myself in and was along for the ride.

Ronald had planned an elaborate proposal, he'd gotten his best friend, Norman to pick me up after work and take me to Rosslyn, VA. We met at the tidal basin, here in DC. It's

Surviving Her – Finding Hope Beyond the Pain

not only a tourist attraction but considered a very romantic place in the evening with the neighboring attractions like the U.S. Capitol and Lincoln Memorial. When Ronald arrived, I was blindfolded. Arm in hand, we walked down the tidal basin, he sat me down on a bench and removed my blindfold. Ronald was on one knee. After hearing his deepest, innermost pleas for my hand in marriage, the girl who wanted it all - the marriage, house, cars, trips around the world, children… said YES. Within twenty-two months, we welcomed another beautiful baby girl. Ronald and I never lived together, although we'd gotten engaged and planned to marry.

There I was, 21 years young, mother of two, engaged and unhappy. There was a swift decline in our relationship after the birth of our second daughter. He became distant. The man who once gave me cards and flowers, dinner dates and movies, every week expressing his love for me, no longer did that. He stopped communicating with me which as they say if he wasn't talking to me; he was

Chiezda Washington

certainly talking to someone else. He became short-tempered and would yell and curse at me, saying hurtful things like "no one will ever love you or want you with two kids." The man I once trusted with my heart was now lying to me too. His usual whereabouts were no longer usual. I'd call his mom's house, where he'd say he was and she'd lie for him. We went from vacations, weekend getaways, dinners out and movies, to barely speaking and only hanging out with family and our children.

Ronald began physically assaulting me. I remember the first time like it was yesterday. A summer evening, I was sitting on my front porch while the kids were inside asleep, and without warning, he showed up at my house. This night, I was having a conversation with my neighbors, who just happen to be a few fraternity boys, and they were like neighborhood brothers. Ronald pulled up, parked his car, and headed inside of my apartment. As he was walking by me, I said, "Go inside, I'll meet you there." When I said that, it pissed him off. He thought the conversation with

Surviving Her — Finding Hope Beyond the Pain

my neighbors was about him because as soon as he pulled up, everyone, including me got quiet. Ronald took his size 9 ½ Timberland boot and forcefully kicked me in my thigh. I let out a muffled scream and jumped to my feet. When my neighbors saw this, they immediately ran over and asked if I needed any help. I told them I didn't. We went inside where he cursed and choked me. I had never been choked by anyone and was truly fighting him off me. He finally let me go and when he did, I fell to the floor to catch my breath. He kept calling me a whore and accusing me of cheating on him. "I know you want to f--- him if you haven't already," he said. All the commotions woke up our daughter, so I told him he had to leave, or I would call the police. So, he left.

After that incident, Ronald and I hadn't seen one another for about six weeks because I'd simply had enough. We talked on the phone occasionally but the man I was still engaged to became a stranger to me just like that. Eventually, he came around trying to apologize, but they

Chiezda Washington

were empty promises. Especially when his temper reared its ugly head when he pushed me during a verbal exchange in my living room. I struck back and left him with eight stitches from a kitchen knife to his abdomen, to remind him of the trauma he'd caused me. It was strike or be struck, and I chose to strike. It wasn't my proudest moment, but I had invested too much time with someone who knew in his heart that he had no good intentions for me and our family. As a woman, I knew what I brought to the table, the very qualities that he once loved about me, had now become the things he despised about me. I was strong, intelligent, beautiful, articulate, driven, self-sufficient, loving, and a monogamous lover. I just couldn't imagine dealing with someone who could hurt me like he did. I no longer respected him, nor did I feel safe around him. I left Ronald after that.

Now, I am a single parent of a 4- and 2-year-old grieving the loss of my relationship, losing my children's father in their lives, and losing my pipe dream. Ronald's words and

Surviving Her – Finding Hope Beyond the Pain

actions had cut me so deeply. I smiled on my job but got home and cried myself to sleep many nights.

I have moved on…. the thought alone was scary, but I had two beautiful little girls to take care of and Ronald was an all-or-nothing kind of person so when I left him; he would not help me, co-parent. So, I have raised them alone, not knowing what tomorrow would hold, but I knew who held tomorrow. I had to constantly tell myself that I was equipped to love my girls and that they would lack nothing, despite their father being absent.

What I had to learn was that domestic violence isn't just physical, it's also emotional, financial, spiritual, and psychological. I asked myself this one simple question, "If I stay and my daughters grow up and ask me if I was happy, what would my answer be?" I had nothing, crickets. There was no way I was willing to stay in a relationship that was tearing me down, crushing my esteem, and almost took my sanity.

Chiezda Washington

The road to releasing all the hurt and pain is going to be an uphill battle, but I know it can be conquered. I believe no mountain can be climbed without rough rocks securing your foothold. I moved away from the area where Ronald and I were together - I needed a brand-new start. This helped me to meet new friends who were not aware of my past and who would get to know the new me. Relocation may not be the answer for you and your family, but you will need to forgive yourself for the experience you have endured but don't place blame on yourself. None of us are aware of how the people in our lives will change during the relationship. We are all just trusting that when and if a change occurs, we are affected in the least way possible. That isn't the case for us all. So, keep your chin up, your shoulders back, and never let your crown slip.

Finding HOPE beyond the pain of this relationship meant that I had to be okay with loving me if no one ever would. I had put so much of myself into that relationship that by the end, I had lost a big part of myself. So, I began

Surviving Her — Finding Hope Beyond the Pain

to journal to help heal my mind and heart of the trauma I'd experienced. I was once stagnant in my dealings with people because I didn't know how to trust anyone else with my heart. The pain of being physically and emotionally betrayed by the person I loved left scars that no one saw but I felt. Several relationships would follow that took a lot of work getting through, but the work was worth it. This led me on an even deeper journey to becoming a Certified Holistic Life Coach. The skills I learned in that certification program have helped me to become clear about my wants and needs and also how to communicate both of those things to others. I'm more assertive, a better listener, and an even better person because of it.

Today, I have a wonderful, full life, great friends, two beautiful adult daughters who are independent, educated, and awesome. I have a new love that gives me exactly what I need. He embodies everything that I manifested through prayer, fasting, and preparation. I'm a Real Estate Agent

Chiezda Washington

with big plans for my future. My oldest daughter graduated from Philadelphia University with a Fashion Degree, and my youngest daughter has a cosmetology license and is working toward purchasing her first home soon. How did I end up so lucky? It wasn't luck at all. It was God who kept me and allowed me to heal.

After all the dust settled, I looked up and was living again. I run a health coaching business named Health Ambassadors, Ltd., that allows me to help others achieve their personal wellness goals and to become health ambassadors for their families. It's fulfilling work as we must identify and conquer the fears we have regarding food, pre-existing family curses and so much more. Some results they can achieve having worked with me is learning new ways to honor themselves using self-care techniques such as journaling, and at-home spa experiences that are deeper than just lighting candles. Clients learn how supplements support their bodies during high-stress times

Surviving Her — Finding Hope Beyond the Pain

and also to be more aware of the rest they are giving to or denying their bodies.

I pray my story helps anyone who is stuck between deciding to stay or leave an abusive situation. This person is asking themselves "Why can't I get the love that I deserve?" The answer is you will find it but not in the person who is hurting you. Remember, love is many things, but it isn't hurtful. We must not negotiate with our happiness. You are responsible to create a world that feeds your soul and you should rarely need an escape from it (outside of the well-deserved vacations to exotic places around the world). You are the co-creator of your destiny and you deserve every good thing that you can imagine for your life.

TIP: Identify what your non-negotiable relationship needs are. The things that you desire to have in your next relationship that if not found, will not be fulfilling and will cause a change of heart. Love, honor, respect, communication, trust, and loyalty are non-negotiables for

Chiezda Washington

me. Think about and create your own and make sure they are in place to serve and protect you.

I want to encourage you to be fearless in your decision to create the best life for yourself and your family. My greatest hope for humanity is that we learn to love one another, without the expectation of perfection. We are all the sum totals of our life experiences and choices. Some of which we can control and others we cannot. You deserve to have a wonderful, peaceful, prosperous, and joyous life!

I'll leave with my favorite quote:

"The greatest weapon formed against fear is *action*." - Chiezda Washington

Website: healthambassadorsltd.com
Facebook @chiezdawashington
Instagram @born_to_win_1216
Email: chiezda@gmail.com

Made in the USA
Columbia, SC
10 September 2020